LIFE DURING THE GREAT CIVILIZATIONS

The Aztec Empire

Sheila Wyborny

BLACKBIRCH®
PRESS

THOMSON

GALE

San Diego • Detroit • New York • San Francisco • Cleveland • New Haven, Conn. • Waterville, Maine • London • Munich

LIBRARY OF CONGRESS CATALOGING-IN-PUBLICATION DATA

Wyborny, Sheila, 1950-
  The Aztec empire / by Sheila Wyborny.
     p. cm. — (Life during the great civilizations)
  Includes bibliographical references and index.
  Contents: The rise and fall of the Aztec empire — Society and laws — Aztec technology
— Religion — Aztec families.
   ISBN 1-56711-736-8 (hardcover : alk. paper)
   1. Aztecs—History—Juvenile literature. 2. Aztecs—Social life and customs—Juvenile
literature. [1. Aztecs. 2. Indians of Mexico.] I. Title. II. Series.

  F1219.73.W93 2004
  972'.018—dc21   2003011409

Printed in United States
10 9 8 7 6 5 4 3 2 1

Contents

The Rise and Fall of the Aztec Empire

The Aztecs once lived in northern Mexico, but around the year 1100, the Aztecs, also called the Mexica, began a long journey south to central Mexico. No one knows exactly why. They arrived in the Valley of Mexico in 1345 and settled on the little land there that was uninhabited. According to legend, on this spot an eagle perched on a cactus with a snake in its talons. This was a sign that the Aztecs had found their new home, a sign that had been foretold by their ancestors.

The Aztecs and other groups in the area had to pay tribute, similar to taxes, to the Tepanecs, a powerful tribe that ruled the area. Had they not, the Aztecs and other, weaker tribes would have been chased away or killed. In about 1428, the Aztecs united with the other tribes in the area and defeated the Tepanecs. By the 1430s, the Aztecs had become so powerful that other tribes paid tribute to them.

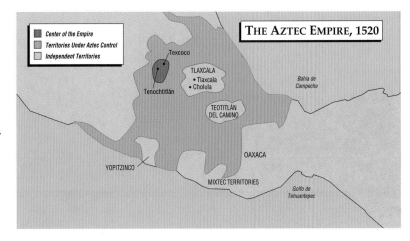

Opposite Page: According to legend, an eagle with a serpent in its talons perched on a cactus and showed the Aztecs their new home in the Valley of Mexico.

The site the Aztecs lived on when they first arrived in the Valley of Mexico was a small island in Lake Texcoco, and with their new wealth, they began to build a great city, which was named Tenochtitlán. Over time, the Aztecs conquered the entire valley, and Tenochtitlán became the capital of the Aztec empire. By the early 1500s, the Aztecs had developed a highly structured and complex society with a strict system of laws that governed the daily lives of its citizens. One Aztec ruler, Montezuma II, also known as Moctezuma, came to power in 1502, when Aztec society was at its peak. Montezuma led an empire of 10 million people that stretched from the Pacific coast to the Gulf of Mexico to the Valley of Mexico.

Spanish explorers and soldiers led by Hernan Cortes arrived in Central America in 1519. They had with them horses, animals never seen before in Mexico. Cortes realized that the Aztecs feared the animals and told his soldiers: "Do you know, gentlemen, that it seems to me that the Indians are terrified at the horses . . . and may think that they and the cannon alone make war on them."[1]

According to Aztec prophesy, gods would come from the west to rule the Aztecs. The Spaniards had come from the west, and the date of their arrival coincided with the one prophesied. Bernal Diaz, one of Cortes's Spanish soldiers, wrote about it in his journal: "[Their] Indian

This Mexican painting shows Lake Texcoco and Tenochtitlán, the capital city of the Aztec empire.

ancestors had foretold that men with beards would come from the direction of the sun and rule over them."[2]

Since Montezuma believed that the Spaniards were gods, the Aztecs did not defend themselves when Cortes arrived. His men freely entered Tenochtitlán and took Montezuma prisoner. At one point, the Spaniards opened fire on the Aztecs in Tenochtitlán during a religious ceremony. The unprovoked attack angered the Aztecs, who killed many of the soldiers. The rest of the soldiers fled the city. Cortes, however, returned several days later with more troops and defeated the Aztecs.

War alone did not destroy the Aztec empire. Although many were killed by the soldiers, the majority of Aztecs who died after the Spanish arrived succumbed to smallpox, a deadly disease the Spaniards brought with them from Europe. While the Spaniards had some immunity to the highly contagious disease, the Aztecs had none. Millions died from their exposure to it.

By 1521, the Aztec empire, which had lasted nearly a hundred years, was defeated. It left a legacy that rivaled that of some European nations, a culture that continues to influence artists, and descendants who proudly acknowledge their connection to its illustrious past.

Although Montezuma welcomed Spanish explorer Hernan Cortes to Tenochtitlán, Cortes took the Aztec leader prisoner.

CHAPTER ONE

Aztec Society

During the 150 years between the Aztecs' arrival in the Valley of Mexico and the height of their empire, they developed a society made up of several distinct social classes with strict laws that governed the people, even the ruling class that wielded the power. Although they were in the minority, the ruling-class nobles had total control over the society.

Nobility and Privilege

The nobles were at the very top of the Aztec social order, and the highest-ranking noble was the *tlahtoani*, a title meaning "he who speaks." The *tlahtoani* was looked upon by all of the other Aztecs as a god-king and was treated with reverence. Bernal Diaz, a Spaniard who came into contact with Aztec society in 1519, wrote that "not one of these chieftains dared even to think of looking [at the *tlahtoani*] in the face but kept their eyes lowered with great reverence."[3]

Although not treated as reverently as the *tlahtoani*, the members of the *tecuhtli*, the preeminent Aztec social order, were also privileged nobles. They were the major landowners, and they managed their property with the assistance of other nobles, who were called *pipiltin*. The *tecuhtli* nobles also held important positions as government officials and military advisers.

Opposite Page: Besides holding important positions in government, nobles in Aztec society were also the greatest warriors.

Priests, like the
one depicted in
this fresco, were
nobles who
interpreted the
sacred calendar
to decide when
to plant crops
or go to war.

Another Aztec social class of nobles were the priests, who served
in the temples and were also trained as interpreters of the sacred Aztec
calendar. The Aztecs believed that their calendar could predict things
such as the best days for planting crops and starting new businesses.
The Aztecs would not start a war unless the calendar predicted success
on the battlefield.

The greatest warriors were also nobles, many of whom were for-
merly commoners, a lower social class. Warriors who distinguished
themselves in battle were sometimes rewarded with tracts of land and
occasionally became *tecuhtli*. Diaz, who witnessed the Aztecs' skill

during battle, described their fierceness and courage: "How they began to charge on us! What a hail of stones sped from their slings! As for the bowmen, the javelins lay like corn on the threshing floor."[4]

Another high-ranking noble was the *tlahtoani*'s top adviser, a male who held the title Cihuacohuatl, which means "snake woman." The Cihuacuhuatl wielded great influence in Aztec society and helped to develop and enforce the city's laws, levied taxes, and controlled the distribution of food.

Commoners who fought bravely in battle sometimes became tecuhtli *who held important positions as military advisers.*

Commoners and Slaves

The nobles had absolute control of the empire, but the Aztec culture would not have survived without the work of the commoners and the toil of the slaves. The Aztec commoners were merchants, craftsmen, and farmers. The merchants and craftsmen passed their skills and knowledge down to their sons, and landowning farmers passed their property down to their children. The craftsmen, who lived in their own section of town, worshiped their own gods and kept to themselves, except when they conducted business. When gold, rare feathers, or precious stones came into the city as tributes, the craftsmen fashioned

Three-fourths of the Aztec population were farmers. These commoners tended the crops that fed the entire empire.

Battle Dress

Some high-ranking warriors wore armor designed to look like an eagle's head and wings.

To protect their bodies during battle, warriors wore armor made of quilted cotton that had been soaked in brine. The fabric of these suits was more than an inch thick and was fashioned into knee-length pants and a single-piece upper-body covering. This tough fabric protected warriors from lances and arrows. High-ranking warriors, such as Jaguar and Eagle Knights, wore ornamentation on their armor.

Jaguar and Eagle Knights were warriors who distinguished themselves in battle. For their battle dress, Jaguar Knights wore the skins of ocelots. The ocelot's head was pulled over the head of the knight so that he looked through the ocelot's jaws. Eagle Knights wore helmets shaped like an eagle's head.

For additional protection, warriors carried shields. Twenty to thirty inches in diameter, the shields were made from wooden frames covered with leather. Nobles carried elaborate shields that were inlaid with gold and turquoise.

them into elaborate jewelry, colorful headdresses, and jeweled and feathered cloaks for the highest-ranking nobles.

The merchants traveled throughout the empire to barter goods. Because they journeyed so widely, the *tlahtoani* sometimes used them as spies and had them gather information. The merchants were secretive people and, when in their own city, kept close to their homes. The merchants lives were relatively easy, which was not the case for the Aztec farmers.

Farmers made up about three-fourths of the Aztec population. They tilled cultivated fields and provided food for the empire. Not only did they feed their families and the empire, they also produced enough crops to pay taxes to the Aztec government.

The life of an Aztec farmer was difficult, with long workdays, but it was not as hard as the life of an Aztec slave. Aztec slaves were usually captured warriors from other tribes or persons who were sold into slavery in order to pay their debts. Slaves performed hard labor and were used to build homes for nobles, public buildings, temples, and roads. Although slaves were at the very bottom of the Aztec social order, they did have some rights. They could, for example, marry free Aztecs, buy their way out of slavery, and own land. Aztec law said that the children of slaves were born free, which broke the cycle of bondage.

Aztec Law

Nobles, slaves, and commoners were all subject to the same laws. Justice in Aztec society was enforced by the *tlahtoani*, who ensured that cases were tried within eighty days. More than eighty laws and consequences for breaking them were recorded in Aztec books. The Aztecs had laws that covered everything from violent crime to gambling to drunkenness. Punishment was swift and harsh if a law was broken. Some laws even dictated the clothing people of the different classes wore.

The laws that governed clothing were carefully spelled out and strictly enforced. Only nobles could wear color-trimmed cloaks, and commoners were restricted to wearing plain clothing. A commoner who wore decorated clothing in public or a cloak below the knee could be put to death. The secretive merchants found a way around this law. In public, they dressed the same as the poor, but at home they wore fine clothing. By wearing their finery only at home, they avoided risking their lives.

Death was the punishment for many crimes. For example, corn, beans, and squash were planted along roadsides to feed the poor, and

Laws governing clothing were very strict. If a commoner wore fancy clothing, like the headdress pictured here, he could be put to death.

Aztec Craftsmen

Some Aztecs were masons, goldsmiths, and craftsmen. They carved beautifully ornamented statues of gods, animals, rulers, and great warriors. They also sculpted blocks into pictures of animals and battle scenes, which were then

The work of Aztec sculptors adorned temples (pictured) and other important buildings.

used to decorate important buildings, such as temples and palaces. Aztec craftsmen also carved stone bowls into the shapes of animals and plants. Some craftsmen worked in stone and clay, but others worked with valuable materials.

Gold was one such medium in which Aztec craftsmen displayed their talents. Artists made gold masks and jewelry for men and women of the noble class. One technique the goldsmiths employed was called the lost-wax process. First, a model of an object was sculpted in clay. The sculpted clay was then covered with wax and another layer of clay was added on top of it. When the model was heated, the wax melted and was poured out. Next, molten gold was poured into the cavity created by the "lost" wax. When the gold cooled, the goldsmith broke the mold to release the gold casting.

if a person took them but was not poor, that person could be executed. Anyone who broke laws that protected the forests could also be killed. While it was legal to remove deadwood from the forest floor, cutting down a live tree without the permission of the landowner was punishable by death.

All crimes carried punishments, but different classes were punished differently for the same offenses. Better behavior was expected from nobles than from other classes. Consequently, nobles were punished more severely for criminal acts. A commoner convicted of public drunkenness had his head shaved and his home destroyed, for example, but a noble convicted of drunkenness was put to death.

Aztec society was a complex social structure with strict laws and harsh consequences for breaking them, and roles were clearly defined among the classes. As diligent as the Aztecs were in following the laws by which they were governed, they were even more obedient to their religion.

CHAPTER TWO

Religion

The Aztecs' temples were among their greatest marvels. Diaz was amazed by their great size and ornamentation. He wrote, "They led us to some large houses [temples] very well built of masonry . . . and on the walls were figured the bodies of many great serpents and other pictures of evil-looking idols. These walls surround a sort of altar. . . . On the other side of the idols were symbols like crosses, and all were colored. At this we stood wondering, as they were things never seen or heard of before."[5]

Every morning, priests stood at the top of the Great Temple pyramid at Tenochtitlán and blew conch shells. This ritual awakened the Aztecs and reminded them that, once again, their gods had favored them and allowed a new day to begin. This was only one of the many rituals that governed the daily lives of Aztecs of all ages. From the time they were young, Aztecs took an active role in the religious rites of their culture.

Becoming a Priest

Although the young daughters of some nobles worked at the temples, and a few of these girls became priestesses, it was mostly the boys who became leaders in the Aztec religion. At the age of eight, the brightest boys were sent to the *calmecac*, the training school for priests. The boys ate only tortillas and water and often fasted for several days at a time. At night, they slept on bare floors, and twice each evening the boy priests

Opposite Page: Priests performed many religious rituals at the giant temples of Tenochtitlán. Religion was an important part of everyday life in the Aztec empire.

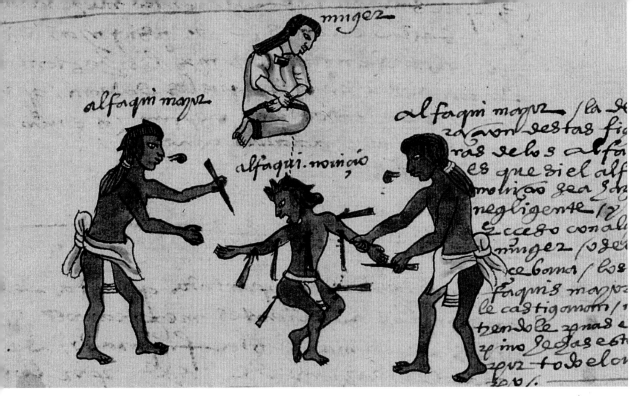

Their training required boy priests to undergo a painful piercing ritual (pictured). The ritual demonstrated the young priests' devotion to their gods.

were awakened to pray and to gather insects needed to make black body paint for the temple's priests.

During one painful ritual, the boys studying to become priests pierced their own tongues and ears with thorns. To please their gods, they had to endure the pain without complaint. In addition to living an austere life, boy priests were carefully trained in a number of skills.

The boy priests studied astronomy, reading, and writing, and learned about medicinal plants. They also memorized songs and the prayers to their many gods. At the age of twenty, the young priests were permitted to leave the temple school if they chose to. If they left, they were free to marry and might become palace scribes or healers, or they could use the astronomy they had learned and become interpreters of sacred books, reference works used to predict the future. Whether the boy priests remained to serve in the temple as priests or went out into society and married, their many gods still profoundly influenced their daily lives.

Aztec Gods and Goddesses

The Aztecs worshiped and feared their gods. They had almost sixteen hundred of them and believed that they affected everything from routine daily life to the elements of nature: earth, wind, rain, and fire. One of the most important gods was Tezcatlipoca, who controlled the fates of all Aztecs. Tlazolteotl, an earth goddess, was associated with childbirth and other new life.

In addition to their gods and goddesses, the Aztecs adopted Quetzalcoatl, the god of learning, from the Toltec tribe. Xochipilli, the Prince of Flowers, was an important god of the Aztecs who was worshiped in colorful community ceremonies.

Festivals and Ceremonies

Aztec public ceremonies that honored the gods were celebrated at least every twenty days, as specified by their calendar. The Aztecs honored their gods diligently because, according to Aztec religion, the gods had sacrificed themselves to make the Sun. Because of this sacrifice, the

An Aztec manuscript depicts Quetzalcoatl and Tezcatlipoca as terrifying gods who devour humans.

Aztecs felt it was their duty to feed the gods. The Aztec priests offered the gods so-called sacred water, which was actually the blood of sacrificial victims.

Human sacrifice was performed to please the gods, keep the Aztec people obedient, and to terrify enemies. Some Aztecs were willing to give their lives to their gods. Before they went to the altar for sacrifice, many adults and children were given strong sedatives. Other victims, however, were captured enemies, and for them it was a horrific event. "Some of the captives were weeping, some were keening, and others were beating their palms against their mouths,"[6] reads one Aztec account.

Human sacrifice was only one element of an Aztec ceremony. The people loved to dance and play music. Drums were made out of wood and clay and covered with animal skins, and flutes and whistles were carved out of wood. Songs and dances were performed at religious ceremonies to please the gods, who in turn would aid the growth of crops throughout the year.

The New Fire ceremony was celebrated every fifty-two years. At the end of this time period, all fires in the empire were extinguished, most household belongings were

The Aztecs sacrificed captured enemies to please the gods and frighten other adversaries.

thrown away, and homes and businesses were carefully scrubbed from top to bottom. After this was done, a victim was sacrificed and his heart removed. Then, priests started a fire in the victim's empty chest cavity. From this fire, torches were lit and carried throughout the empire to start new fires in each community, business, and household. This would begin the new fifty-two-year period.

Personal Rituals

Although everyone attended the New Fire ceremony, other rituals were simple affairs, held in private homes. Each household marked the major events in the lives of family members with small religious ceremonies. Niches in walls held images of household gods, which Aztecs

The Sacred Calendar Stone of Tenochtitlán

At twenty-four tons and twelve feet across, the Calendar Stone of Tenochtitlán is the largest known Aztec carving. At the calendar's center is Tonatiuh, the Sun. Tonatiuh is flanked by claws that grip human hearts. The top of the outermost panel is inscribed with the date "13 Reed." According to Aztec religion, this was the date when the present Sun was born. On the four rectangular panels in the central zone are the dates when the previous suns were destroyed. The inner circle is carved with the twenty signs that represent the days of the month. Day signs had different qualities. These signs, and the date of the month on which a person was born,

Aztec priests used the sacred Calendar Stone (pictured) to predict the best times to wage war, plant crops, and perform other important tasks.

were supposed to influence both the personality traits and the future of the person.

worshiped daily. Families performed rituals to mark the births and naming of babies, when members began or finished schooling, and, of course, weddings.

The marriage ceremony was a private family affair. A matchmaker married the couple by tying the corners of their cloaks together. Afterward, the bride, groom, and their families sang, danced, and feasted. Aztecs generally married for life.

At the end of life, the dead were ritualistically prepared at home to enter the next world. The dead were carefully bathed and dressed in their best clothes. Even after death, children and infants were still considered a part of the family. They were buried under the floor or in the yard next to the house. Not all Aztecs were buried, however; some were cremated.

All of the dead were equipped with grave goods, possessions to help them in the afterlife. Sometimes grieving relatives held ceremonies up to four years after the loved one's death. As with most household ceremonies, the funeral was presided over by a shaman.

A shaman, a sort of local part-time priest, visited homes to lead celebrations, to conduct ceremonies that would solve daily problems, or to assist healers to cure illness. A shaman could predict the survival or the death of a patient by tying knots into a cord that he yanked tightly. If the sick person could untie the cord, he or she would recover; if the knot could not be untied, the Aztecs believed the person would die.

Aztecs obeyed the demands of their gods, who they thought affected many aspects of existence, but they also worked to improve their lives. During the relatively short life of their empire, the Aztecs developed many technological and scientific innovations, some of which were more sophisticated than those of their European counterparts.

CHAPTER THREE

Aztec Science and Technology

When the Aztecs first arrived in the Valley of Mexico in 1345, it was an inhospitable land. They lived on frogs and fish and bartered with other tribes for firewood. The Aztecs were resourceful people, though, and improved their living conditions. In particular, advances in communication led to defenses that allowed Aztec culture to mature.

Communications and Record Keeping

As the Aztec empire grew, its rulers needed to know what was happening in their territory, and they needed to know if enemies threatened invasion. Since there were no communication systems or forms of transportation other than the canoe, the Aztec rulers had to rely on foot messengers, men who could keep the rulers informed about events throughout the empire. Not only did messengers have to be physically fit, they also needed to have a good memory.

To Montezuma, one event was so important that he entrusted his most elite warriors, called Jaguar Knights, rather than his palace messengers, to obtain information. The arrival of the Spaniards was reported by a messenger and recorded in an Aztec document: "[Montezuma] sent five messengers to greet the strangers and to bring them gifts. . . . He said unto them: 'Come forward, my Jaguar Knights, come forward. It is said that

Opposite Page: This illustration depicts the Aztec migration from northern Mexico to the Valley of Mexico farther south.

Aztec written language used small picture symbols called glyphs, which were recorded in books called codices.

our lord has returned to this land. Go to meet him. Go to hear him. Listen to what he tells you; listen and remember.'"[7]

The Jaguar Knights carried out their duties and reported back to Montezuma in person. Most messengers, however, worked in relays, with documents and messages being passed along to new messengers at relay stations spaced about five or six miles apart. For a civilization with no form of land transportation, this became the most reliable means of communication.

The Aztec empire's messenger system for communication was primitive at best, as was the written language that developed and was used to document important historical events, religious ceremonies, business transactions, and the events of daily life. Aztec writing consisted of small picture symbols called glyphs that looked like colorful pictures. Samples of this writing were recorded in books the Aztecs called codices. The writing in these codices provide much of what is known about Aztec culture.

The scribes who kept the records contained in the codices were members of the noble class. They were highly trained craftsmen who also created the pigments used to paint the colorful glyphs and knew the many picture symbols of the Aztec written language. Although young priests were trained in the written language at the temple school, the acquisition of these skills was so time-consuming and difficult that scribes were often hereditary positions.

Agriculture

Farming was another job that succeeding generations of a family would perform. The farmers of the Aztec empire had no work animals, farm carts, or plows. Instead, they turned the soil with digging sticks, a farming tool that served as both spade and hoe. As the Aztec population grew, the farmers developed more sophisticated agricultural techniques to help produce more food.

Farmers cultivated their crops using simple tools like the digging stick, which functioned as both a spade and a hoe.

Farmers terraced steep hillsides to plant more crops and used irrigation to bring water from springs, which vastly increased the amount of food they could grow. To do this, the Aztecs built carefully planned canals. The excavation of the canals and the construction of dams to store water required heavy labor.

Developing irrigation systems was not a one-time effort. Canal systems had to be maintained to keep them from filling with silt, and the entire community was enlisted in the effort to keep them

flowing. The improvement of farming techniques reduced the number of people required for farming while it produced greater quantities of food for the growing population. This in turn freed many members of Aztec society to pursue other discoveries, such as those that were made in the field of medicine.

Health Care

These glyphs show how Aztec healers set broken bones and cured fevers. Aztec medical skills often surpassed those of Spanish doctors of the time.

Although many Aztec ideas about medicine and illness were a blend of magic and religion, many of their treatments, such as massage and heat for the treatment of injuries, had a scientific basis.

Aztec healers made house calls to the homes of sick and injured people, and categorized more than a thousand different herbs to be used medicinally. In fact, the medical skills of the Aztecs were more advanced in many ways than those of Spanish doctors of the period. For example, Aztec healers could stitch wounds and set broken bones in plaster casts, which were reinforced by splints. Setting bones in casts was a medical technique not yet used by the Spaniards.

Making Cities Better Places to Live

The Aztecs' well-managed cities were, in many ways, also superior to their Spanish equivalents.

Medicinal Herbs

Aztec healers used Indian turnip (pictured) to treat stomach ailments.

The Aztecs used hundreds of herbs medicinally. Some were taken internally in teas or powders, some were burned for their scents, and some were used as ointments. The Aztec lily and jimsonweed were used by Aztecs to reduce fever. Jimsonweed, however, is poisonous and had to be administered in carefully measured doses. Stomach problems were treated with Indian turnip, also known as jack-in-the-pulpit. Juniper was used to aid in the recovery of muscle and tendon injuries, as well as to ease the pain of arthritis and rheumatism. Some herbs, though, were strictly ceremonial in nature, such as peyote, which was ingested to induce hallucinogenic visions.

The Aztec cities were known for their cleanliness, with sparkling buildings and streets kept free of debris.

The great city of Tenochtitlán was designed to expedite the flow of travelers and to protect the city from invaders. The Aztecs built three large causeways across Lake Texcoco to connect the island city to the lake's shores. The causeways, which were guarded by soldiers, permitted Aztecs to enter and leave the city yet kept out their enemies.

Besides walking, the Aztecs' only form of transportation was the canoe. Canals dug through Tenochtitlán allowed canoes of different sizes to navigate the city. Spanish soldiers were surprised by the size of some of the canoes they saw. Diaz described some of the bigger ones: "The canoes were large ones made like hollow troughs cleverly cut from huge single logs, and many of them would hold forty Indians."[8]

The Aztecs diverted water for drinking as well as for transportation. They devised aqueduct systems to supply water for people living in the cities. Aqueducts, pipes or channels that direct water from one place to another, were used to control the flow of the water that was brought from the mountains to the cities in canals. Once the water was in the cities, aqueducts carried it to pools and public fountains. People

Canoes were the only kind of transportation through the canals of Tenochtitlán.

collected it in large vessels and took it to their homes. Thanks to the aqueduct system, water was readily available throughout the city.

The Aztec capital of Tenochtitlán had no problems with getting water, since it was built on a lake. The problem with Tenochtitlán was its limited amount of land. When the Aztecs wanted to expand the city, they constructed *chinampas*, small man-made islands. A *chinampa* might be as small as five feet across or as large as fifty feet. A wooden framework was covered with a mat, and mud from the lake bed was piled onto the mat. Willow trees, which were planted at the corners of the *chinampa*, sent down deep roots and anchored it in place. Some *chinampas* were so sturdy that houses were built on them, and others were made into gardens. Very large *chinampas* were planted with crops.

The *chinampas* improved the lives of the Aztecs by making food more readily available in the city. Other improvements, such as their structures built without the use of modern tools, are feats of engineering. Proof of their engineering and technological sophistication is also evident in the construction of their larger temples of worship and the palaces of wealthy families.

The Aztecs built small islands, called chinampas *(pictured), in Lake Texcoco when they needed to expand Tenochtitlán.*

CHAPTER FOUR

How the Aztecs Lived

The Aztecs were family oriented people who worshiped and celebrated major events together. Also, many families would work together to achieve common goals. Whether the Aztecs lived in fine palaces or simple huts, home and family were vitally important to them.

Homes

The most powerful Aztec nobles lived in great luxury in huge palaces. Montezuma's palace, for instance, had one hundred rooms and one hundred baths. Its walls were made of marble, and the courtyards were filled with fountains, flowers, and songbirds.

Lesser nobles lived in multistoried palaces with rooms built around central plazas, which were also planted with flowers. Furniture was sparse, and everyone—except for priests in training—slept on mats on the floor. To keep warm, they covered themselves with blankets in cold weather. Diaz remarked on the sleeping arrangements that the Aztecs provided for the Spaniards: "For every one of us, beds of matting with canopies above, and no better bed is given, however great the chief may be, for they are not used."[9]

Although sleeping arrangements were the same for everybody, homes were not. Commoners' homes were restricted to a single story, and most commoners lived in two-

Opposite Page: Most commoners lived in simple houses that had only two rooms. They worked and ate in one room and slept in the other.

room houses. Commoners ate and worked in one room and slept in the other. The houses were built of mud brick and were not ornate in any way. Some artists and craftsmen, however, had small courtyards, a privilege of their trade. Commoners had little or no furniture, and possessions such as fishing nets, pots, weaving looms, and storage pots were stored at the room's perimeter. The poorest commoners lived in simple huts around the edge of the city and kept turkeys, rabbits, and bees on the land that surrounded their huts. Commoners were not only restricted in the size of their homes but also in the type of clothing they could wear.

Clothing

An Aztec's social class was easily identifiable by his or her clothes. Commoners and slaves wore plain clothing. Men wore loincloths, long strips of cloth wrapped around the waist, pulled up between the legs, and tied in front. They also wore short, sleeveless cloaks. All women wore long skirts and long, sleeveless blouses. The cloaks of commoners had to be shorter than the knees and could only be tied over the right shoulder.

People of the noble class wore long, colorful cloaks decorated with embroidery and feathers. To display their wealth, they sometimes wore more than one cloak. Nobles could choose whether they tied their cloaks over the left shoulder or in front. The material the nobles' clothing was made from was finer than the rough fabric worn by commoners and slaves.

While Aztec nobles (pictured) wore long, colorful, decorated cloaks made from fine fabric, commoners could only wear plain cloaks that fell above their knees.

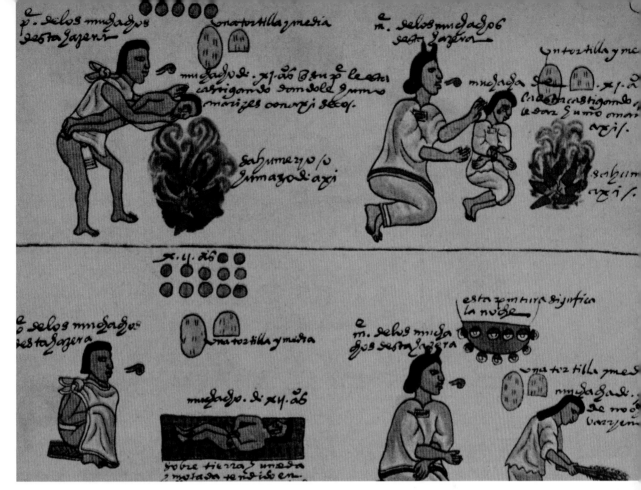

The clothing of female commoners was as plain as that of the men, but noblewomen wore richly embroidered clothing as well as elaborate jewelry, and they sometimes wore makeup, too.

Family Life and Meals

Whether its members were well dressed or not, a family was usually large. Besides the father (called *tahtli*), the mother (*nantli*), and children, an Aztec family might also consist of aunts, uncles, nieces, nephews, and grandparents. In the family of a nobleman, there might be more than one wife. In fact, one *tlahtoani* is said to have had two thousand wives. Regardless of the size of the family, each family member had responsibilities, no matter how old he or she.

Aztec families were usually large, and every member of the family, including young children, had specific chores and responsibilities.

37

Play Ball

The Aztecs played a ball game called *tlachtli*, or hip ball. The balls were made from tree sap. The ball game was a sport as well as part of religious celebrations. The *tlachtli* court symbolized the universe, and the ball represented the Sun or Moon. Only noblemen were allowed to play the game, but everyone was permitted to watch and cheer their favorite teams. The object of the game was for one team to knock the hard ball through its opponent's stone rings, which were hung sideways on a wall and were barely wide enough for the ball to pass through. Players could only use their knees, hips, or elbows to move the ball. This was so difficult to do

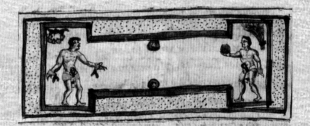

Noblemen played tlachtli *both as a sport and as part of religious celebrations.*

that if a player got the ball through the ring, his team won the game and could demand possessions from the spectators.

As they grew, Aztec children were taught society's rules, the most important of which was that all people were expected to be industrious and hardworking. The children of commoners began to do household chores at the age of three. Boys as young as five carried firewood, and by fourteen, boys fished to help feed their families. Girls had responsibilities as well. At age six, girls were taught to spin thread, and by fourteen, most girls could weave and cook, and had the responsibilities of women. Boys and girls were severely reprimanded if they did not do their chores and learn their lessons.

Between the ages of twelve and fifteen, all boys and girls attended evening lessons at the House of Song, a school where children learned poems, songs, and dances. The early teen years were especially busy for sons of nobles. At fourteen or fifteen, they began a formal education in which they learned the skills necessary to hold important positions. Children also learned lessons from their parents. Most important, they learned from parents how to behave as adults.

An Aztec father was responsible for the well-being of his home and family. By his example, he showed his children how to be thrifty, caring, and courageous. Although he spent much of his time outside the

Spanish conquerors adopted tortillas, pepper-spiced dishes, and other Aztec foods. These popular foods and other elements of Aztec culture remain even though the Aztec empire fell long ago.

house at work, he did join his family for the evening meal, which was prepared by the women.

Women raised children, wove fabric for clothing, prepared meals, and did other housekeeping chores. In addition to household tasks, farmers' wives helped to bring in the harvest and sold surplus farm goods at market. Mothers had help from grandparents in raising the children and attending to household responsibilities.

Grandparents taught children household skills and instructed them about their religion. Children always had the advice and attention of an adult when they needed it. Grandmothers also helped mothers and older daughters prepare meals.

Regardless of their social class, all Aztecs ate with their fingers and carefully washed their hands before and after meals. The diet of most Aztecs consisted of maize, a type of corn; beans; and the occasional duck or crow. Rabbits, turkeys, and dogs were consumed at special events. Other Aztec dishes were steamed pancakes stuffed with fish or tadpoles, and tortillas with tomato and pepper stew.

The wealthy had a greater selection of food. It was said that Montezuma could choose from among a hundred dishes each day. Pig and pheasants were favorites of the noble class, and oysters, crabs, and turtles were also popular. Only the wealthy could afford a delicious drink, made from cacao beans, called *chocolatl* (known today as chocolate). For flavoring, they used honey, spices, or vanilla. Commoners, however, only drank water.

Despite the fact that the Aztec empire fell to Spanish conquerors five hundred years ago, some influences of the Aztec culture persist. The Spanish adopted a number of Aztec foods, such as tortillas and dishes spiced with peppers, which are still popular today. The Spanish also brought examples of Aztec writing and art back to Europe with them, and those examples continue to influence artists. Though Aztec civilization is gone, parts of its culture have endured.

Notes

Introduction: The Rise and Fall of the Aztec Empire

1. Bernal Diaz, *The Discovery and Conquest of Mexico, 1517–1521*, trans. A.P. Maudslay. New York: Farrar, Straus, & Giroux, 1956, p. 61.
2. Diaz, *The Discovery and Conquest of Mexico*, p. 24.

Chapter 1: Aztec Society

3. Diaz, *The Discovery and Conquest of Mexico*, p. 193.
4. Diaz, *The Discovery and Conquest of Mexico*, pp. 130–131.

Chapter 2: Religion

5. Diaz, *The Discovery and Conquest of Mexico*, pp. 9–10.
6. Miguel Leon-Portilla, trans., *The Broken Spears: The Aztec Account of the Conquest of Mexico*, Boston: Beacon, 1992, p. 107.

Chapter 3: Aztec Science and Technology

7. Leon-Portilla, *The Broken Spears*, p. 23.
8. Diaz, *The Discovery and Conquest of Mexico*, p. 6.

Chapter 4: How the Aztecs Lived

9. Diaz, *The Discovery and Conquest of Mexico*, pp. 194–195.
10. Diaz, *The Discovery and Conquest of Mexico*, p. 91.

Glossary

aqueduct: A conduit for moving large quantities of flowing water from one place to another.

calmecac: Training school for priests.

causeway: A raised road that crosses water.

chinampa: A man-made island sturdy enough to support a house. Made by loading lake-bed mud onto a square, matted framework of wood.

codex: An Aztec manuscript.

glyph: A picture used instead of written words.

prophesy: A prediction of a future extent.

smallpox: A highly contagious disease that causes acute skin eruptions and scarring. During the time of the Aztecs, it was the most serious disease in the New World and killed millions.

tlahtoani: The supreme Aztec ruler.

tribute: A payment paid to a stronger, more powerful country by a weaker country.

For More Information

Books

Judith Crosher, *The Aztecs*. Morristown, NJ: Silver Burdett, 1976.

Tami Deedrick, *Aztecs*. Austin, TX: Raintree Streck-Vaughn, 2002.

Jill Hughes, *Aztecs*. New York: Glocester, 1980.

Richard Platt, *Aztecs*: *The Fall of the Aztec Capital*. New York: DK, 1999.

Donna Walsh Shepherd, *The Aztecs*. New York: Franklin Watts, 1992.

Gene S. Smart, *The Mighty Aztecs*. Washington, DC: National Geographic Society, 1981.

Websites

American Indian Heritage Foundation (www.indians.org).
Provides information on Aztec religion and history. Also includes a translation of the Aztec calendar and a listing of emperors and gods.

The Aztecs (www.rose-hulman.edu).

Includes photographs of archaeological sites, Aztec art, and portions of codices. Also illustrated are ball games, events of daily life, and jewelry.

Civilizations in America: The Mexica/Aztecs (www.swu.edu).

Describes the history, social order, economy, and religion of the Aztecs, with photographs of archaeological excavation sites.

Index

Picture Credits

cover © Nik Wheeler/CORBIS; page 4 © The Art Archive/Antochiw Collection
Mexico/Mireille Vautier; page 6 © Charles & Hosette Lenars/CORBIS; pages 7,
12, 29, 37 © Bettmann/CORBIS; page 8 © Stapleton Collection/CORBIS; pages
10, 30, 34 © The Art Archive; page 11 © Archivo Iconografico, S.A./CORBIS;
page 13 © John Bigelow Taylor/Art Resource, NY; page 15 © The Art
Archive/Museum für Völkerkunde vienna/Dagli Orti; pages 16, 31 © Corel
Corporation; page 18 © Neil Beere/CORBIS; page 20 © The Art Archive/Bodleian
Library Oxford/The Bodleian Library; page 21 © Goraudon/Art Resource, NY;
page 22 © Snark/Art Resource, NY; page 23 © Mary Evans/Explorer
Archives/Courau; page 24 © Anthroarcheart.org/Philip Baird; pages 26, 33 ©
Gianni Dagli Orti/CORBIS; page 28 © Werner Forman/Art Resource, NY; pages
32, 39 © The Art Archive/National Archives Mexico/Dagli Orti; pages 36, 38 ©
The Art Archive/Biblioteca Nacional Madrid/Dagli Orti

About the Author

Sheila Wyborny began her writing career after retiring from a Houston, Texas, area school system. She and her husband, Wendell, a broadcast engineer, still live in Houston. They are in the process of building a home in a small subdivision with an attached airfield so they can keep their Cessna 170 aircraft in their own backyard.